Izzy!
Wizzy!

'Izzy Wizzy'
An original concept by Elizabeth Dale
© Elizabeth Dale

Illustrated by Louise Forshaw

Published by MAVERICK ARTS PUBLISHING LTD

Studio 3A, City Business Centre, 6 Brighton Road,

Horsham, West Sussex, RH13 5BB

© Maverick Arts Publishing Limited May 2017

+44 (0)1403 256941

A CIP catalogue record for this book is available at the British Library.

ISBN 978-1-84886-253-1

Maverick
arts publishing
www.maverickbooks.co.uk

Yellow

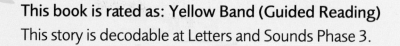

This book is rated as: Yellow Band (Guided Reading)
This story is decodable at Letters and Sounds Phase 3.

Izzy! Wizzy!

by **Elizabeth Dale**
illustrated by **Louise Forshaw**

I am called Izzy, and I am magic.

Look at all my magic spells...

Izzy! Wizzy!

I wish for a cat that I can hug!

Oh no! I cannot hug a slug!

Izzy! Wizzy! I wish for a pet hippo!

Eek! I do not need a pet toad!

Izzy! Wizzy! I wish for a doll to dress up!

No! No! I cannot dress up a snail!

Izzy! Wizzy! I wish for a dog.

No! A fish cannot run with me!

Izzy! Wizzy! I wish for a rabbit.

No! This crab will nip me!

I am no good at magic spells!

Please let this wish work!

Izzy! Wizzy! I wish for a boat, please!

Look! That wish did happen –
and the rest did, too!

Quiz

1. When Izzy wishes for a cat, what does she get?
a) A dog
b) A mouse
c) A slug

2. Why does Izzy want a doll?
a) She wants to hug it
b) She wants to dress it up
c) She wants to swim with it

3. What can't the fish do?
a) Run
b) Swim
c) Blow bubbles

4. Where was the rabbit meant to come out from?
a) A bed
b) A boat
c) A hat

5. Why does Izzy's last wish work?
a) Because she said the magic word "Please!"
b) Because she said "Abra Kadabra!"
c) Because she was hungry

Turn over for answers

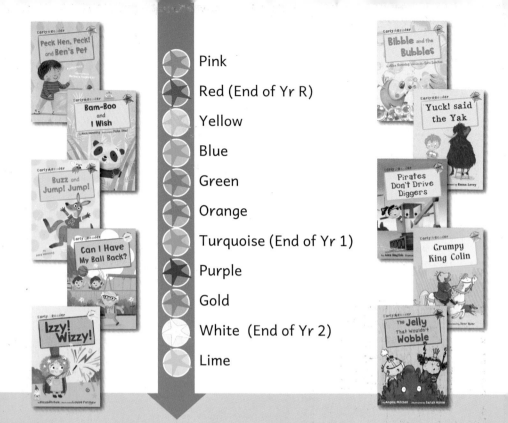

Pink

Red (End of Yr R)

Yellow

Blue

Green

Orange

Turquoise (End of Yr 1)

Purple

Gold

White (End of Yr 2)

Lime

Book Bands for Guided Reading

The Institute of Education book banding system is made up of twelve colours, which reflect the level of reading difficulty. The bands are assigned by taking into account the content, the language style, the layout and phonics.

Children learn at different speeds but the colour chart shows the levels of progression with the national expectation shown in brackets. To learn more visit the IoE website: www.ioe.ac.uk.

All of these books have been book banded for guided reading to the industry standard and edited by a leading educational consultant.

For more titles visit: www.maverickbooks.co.uk/early-readers

Quiz Answers: 1c, 2b, 3a, 4c, 5a